How Artists Use

SHAPE

Paul Flux

www.heinemann.co.uk
Visit our website to find out more information about Heinemann Library books.

To order:

 Phone 44 (0) 1865 888066

 Send a fax to 44 (0) 1865 314091

 Visit the Heinemann Bookshop at www.heinemann.co.uk to browse our catalogue and order online.

First published in Great Britain by Heinemann Library, Halley Court, Jordan Hill, Oxford OX2 8EJ,
a division of Reed Educational and Professional Publishing Ltd.

Heinemann is a registered trademark of Reed Educational and Professional Publishing Ltd.

OXFORD MELBOURNE AUCKLAND JOHANNESBURG BLANTYRE
GABORONE IBADAN PORTSMOUTH (NH) USA CHICAGO

Designed by Celia Floyd
Illustrations by Jo Brooker/Ann Miller
Originated by Ambassador Litho Ltd
Printed and bound by South China Printing in Hong Kong/China

ISBN 0 431 16203 4 (hardback)   ISBN 0 431 16208 5 (paperback)
06 05 04 03 02   06 05 04 03 02
10 9 8 7 6 5 4 3 2 1   10 9 8 7 6 5 4 3 2 1

British Library Cataloguing in Publication Data

Flux, Paul
    How artists use shape. (Take-off!)
    1.Proportion (Art) – Juvenile literature 2.Composition (Art) – Juvenile literature
    I.Title
    701.8

Acknowledgements

The publishers would like to thank the following for permission to reproduce photographs:

AKG, London: pp10, 20 / DACS p11, Eric Lessing Museo Nazionale Naples p9, Kuntsmuseum Berne / DACS p15, National Gallery of Ireland p19; Art Archive: Tate Gallery, London / DACS p21; Bridgeman Art Library: Bolton Museum and Art Gallery, Lancashire / DACS p18, Kunstsammlung Nordrhein-Westfalen, Dusseldorf / DACS p5, National Gallery of Scotland / Duke of Sutherland Collection p12, St. Peter's, Vatican, Rome p17; Trevor Clifford: pp28, 29; Corbis: Philadelphia Museum of Art pp13, 14; M.C.Escher's Fishes and Scales c.2000 Cordon Art B.V.-Baarn-Holland: p8; Giarandon: p7; Henry Moore Foundation: p16; Hermitage, St Petersburg: DACS p24; National Gallery, Scotland / Estate of S. J. Peploe: p26; Tate Picture Library, London: p4.

Cover photograph reproduced with permission of Bridgeman Art Library.

Our thanks to Sue Graves and Hilda Reed for their advice and expertise in the preparation of this book.

Every effort has been made to contact copyright holders of any material reproduced in this book. Any omissions will be rectified in subsequent printings if notice is given to the publishers.

Contents

Any words appearing in the text in bold, **like this**, are explained in the Glossary.

What is shape?

Our world is full of shapes: squares, circles, triangles – even some which have no name. Some artists arrange shapes so that we can recognize objects in their paintings. Others use shape to make **abstract** pictures.

How many different shapes can you see in this picture?

Wyndham Lewis, *Workshop*, 1914–15.

Wassily Kandinsky, *Intersecting Lines*, 1923.

A shape is an **outline**, filled with colour. This picture is full of different shapes. Start at the bottom right-hand corner and look towards the top left-hand corner. We know paintings cannot move, but the shapes look as if they are flying away from us.

Common shapes

circle

oval

triangle

square

hexagon

rectangle

This picture is made up of many different shapes.

An artist draws a line, joins it together and fills in the space with colour. A shape is made! The space around shapes makes other shapes. A picture is a collection of shapes which fit together, like a jigsaw puzzle. Artists can use shape to make us look at a picture in a particular way.

eyes

head

body

The *Mona Lisa* is one of the most famous paintings in the world. It is by the Italian artist Leonardo da Vinci. He lived from 1452 to 1519.

The eyes of the woman in this painting seem to follow you as you move around. The **triangular** shape of the woman leads our eyes up from her body to her head at the top of the painting. This is why we are always drawn back to look at the woman's face.

Shapes make space

Can you estimate how many fish are in this picture?

M. C. Escher,
*Fish and
Scales*, 1959.

In this picture we notice the lines of white fish, but look at the
spaces between them. In the middle are two sets of fish scales.
One set moves upwards, the other down. As our eyes follow
them they change into small fish which get bigger.

A Roman artist made this **mosaic**. It shows all the fish and sea creatures in the water near the old city of Pompeii in Italy. Their shapes are fixed, but the fish seem to wriggle and sway in the water.

A mosaic is a picture made from hundreds of small pieces of coloured glass and **marble**. This mosaic is more than 2000 years old.

Roman mosaic, Pompeii, Italy.   octopus   shell   fish

9

Coloured shapes

The horse in this cave painting has been drawn with a single line and this **outline** has been coloured in with an unusual **shade** of yellow. Around the young horse are shapes, which look like grass, insects or even birds. The artist has captured the movement of a real animal.

outline

Cave painting, Lascaux, France.

Franz Marc, *The Yellow Cow*, 1911.

Here is an animal set in a **landscape** of colourful shapes. This was painted about 90 years ago, much more recently than the picture on page 10. The mixture of solid shapes and bold colours make this a very strong picture.

How shape is used in portraits

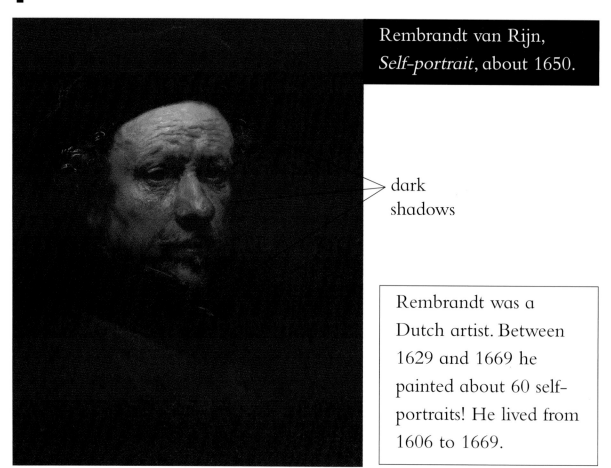

Rembrandt van Rijn, *Self-portrait*, about 1650.

dark shadows

Rembrandt was a Dutch artist. Between 1629 and 1669 he painted about 60 self-portraits! He lived from 1606 to 1669.

In this **portrait** we see the **solid** shape of the artist looking straight back at us. He looks worried, almost sad. The dark shadows show the shape of an unhappy man. When Rembrandt was young he showed himself happy and successful. But at the end of his life, when he was poor, he painted himself like this.

Here the artist has exaggerated shapes to create an unusual effect. In this picture the woman's neck and her small head seem carefully balanced. They contrast with the solid shape of her dark dress. Like the *Mona Lisa* on page 7, the **triangular** shape of the body leads our eyes up to the top of the picture, to the woman's head.

small head

long neck

dark dress

Amedeo Modigliani was an Italian painter and sculptor. He lived from 1884 to 1920.

Amedeo Modigliani, *Portrait of a Polish Woman*, 1919.

How shape is used in landscape

This picture of a few houses bathed in sunlight seems very simple. Yet there is something very special about this painting. The shapes work together to show us a place where people and nature exist side by side.

green trees

roof

house

grey light

Paul Cézanne, *Mont Sainte-Victoire*, 1902-06.

Georges Braque, *Houses at L'Estaque*, 1908.

Many people see Cubism as the start of modern **abstract** painting.

Only a few years later Georges Braque painted a similar **scene**, but in a very different way. Here the buildings are **solid** shapes, broken up by light and shadow. This **style** is now called **Cubism**.

15

Solid shapes – sculpture

Henry Moore made this sculpture in bronze so that it would not fade or rust.

bronze shape

Henry Moore, *Sheep Piece*, 1971-72.

Sculpture is often displayed outside, so it has to look good in many kinds of light. The artist of this **bronze** sculpture has used shape to show the living form of a mother sheep and her lamb. He wanted the sculpture to become part of the **landscape**.

Mary

Jesus

folds of cloth

Michelangelo was Italian and lived from 1475 to 1564. He was not only a painter, but also a sculptor, **architect** and poet!

Look at the folds of cloth and the way the bodies seem to come to life in this sculpture. It does not look like it is made of **marble**, a very hard rock. The **scene** is one the artist has imagined. Mary, the mother of Jesus, cradles Him in her arms after He has been taken down from the cross.

Shapes to make us think

Ben Nicholson was living in Cornwall when he painted this picture. The peaceful **landscape** is made of coloured shapes, each pushing against the next.

Ben Nicholson, *Cornish Landscape*, 1940.

maid

curtain

woman

Do you feel as if you could reach out and pull the curtain across the room?

Here, light floods in through a window, as one woman looks out and another writes at her desk. We are looking at the corner of a room. Although there is a lot of light in the picture, the space seems closed in by strong shapes.

Moving shapes

Kasimir Malevich, *Suprematism*, 1915.

Are the shapes in this picture moving or still? What does this picture make you think about? Try to draw a picture like this yourself.

The Russian artist Kasimir Malevich did not try to show real-life objects in this painting. The shapes and colours work together to create a picture which can make us think of many things. The shapes float in space.

The woman has no colour in her face and eyes. What do you think this means?

Pablo Picasso painted this picture while he was angry about the Spanish Civil War (1936-39). The woman's head is a strange shape, because the grief she is feeling has changed what she looks like. The straight lines of the background show up the twisted shapes of her face to show her emotion.

Drawing using shape outlines

Without **shade** and **detail** some shapes can be confusing and difficult to recognize, while others are very easy. Can you identify the shape **outlines** in this picture?

A drawing of three different cat shapes.

coloured space

cat outline

face details

Try drawing an animal outline picture.

1. Choose an animal and make an outline of it.
2. Draw two more of the same animal in different positions.
3. Cut out the three shapes and arrange them on a piece of paper.
4. Trace round the shapes and add some details.
5. Use different colours in the spaces between the shapes.

Making a picture using simple shapes

Here is a group of buildings painted in a similar **style** to the pictures on pages 14 and 15. The **rectangular** shapes of the houses and roofs make the picture feel **solid**. The blocks of colour make the simple slopes feel strong.

André Derain, *At La Roche Guillon*, 1910.

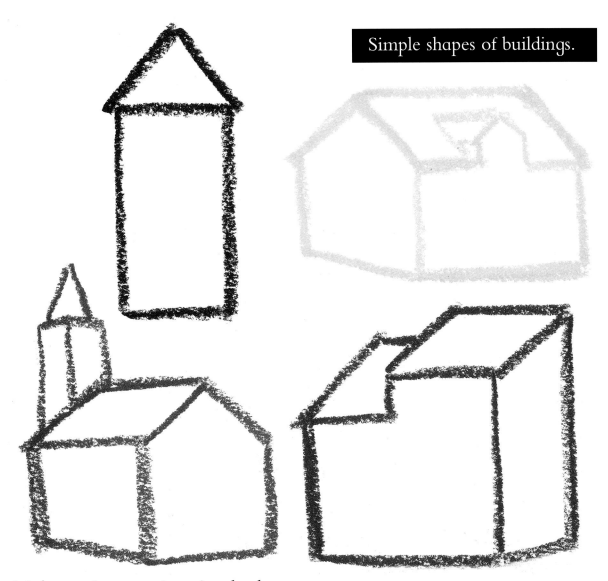

Make a picture using simple shapes.

1. Copy one of these buildings carefully.
2. Colour it in using blocks of colours.
3. Add other shapes until you have made the picture into a complete scene.

25

Using everyday objects

How many shapes can you see in this picture?

Samuel John Peploe, *Still Life*, about 1913.

A picture of everyday objects is called a still life. Many artists enjoy painting this kind of picture because they can make ordinary things look special. Here the shapes and colours of the background are **repeated** in the objects themselves. This makes it difficult to see where one ends and the other begins.

26

Draw your own still life.

1. Arrange three or four simple objects in an interesting way.
2. Draw the outline shapes of the objects. Try this a few times until you get the best view.
3. Draw lines across and down your picture to divide the background space.
4. Colour the shapes and background so that the objects really stand out.

Make a picture book

Make your own **concertina book** like this:

1. Fold a piece of A3 paper into eight rectangles.
2. Open the paper out and fold it again on the longest line.
3. Fold it in half, and then fold one end towards you and the other away from you.
4. Number the pages. Put 1 on the cover, and then 2 to 8 for the rest.

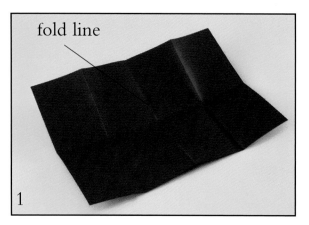

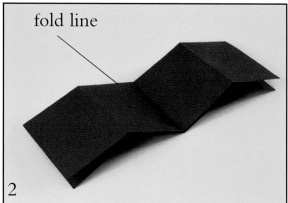

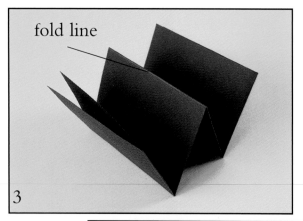

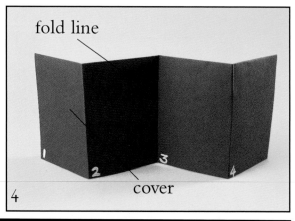

Four pictures showing you how to make a concertina book.

front cover

paper shapes

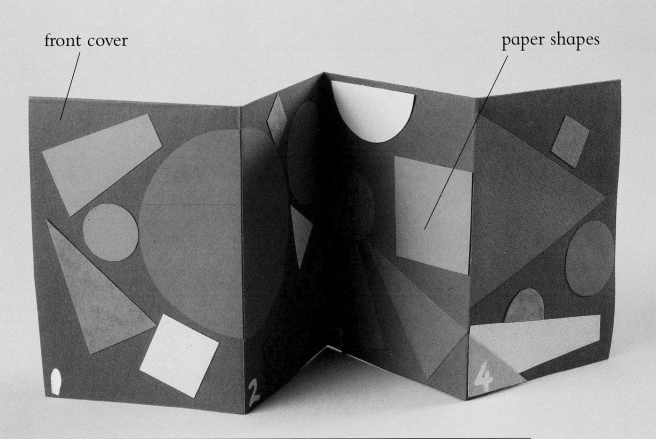

Some of the earliest books were made in China in this way.

Now make some shape pictures for your concertina book:
1. Cut out some paper shapes in different colours and sizes.
2. Make your own **abstract** picture on the cover. Think about how the shapes fit together.
3. **Repeat** the picture on the other pages, but move the shapes around and change their colours and sizes.
4. Finally, think of a good title for the cover.

Glossary

a b c d e f g h i j k l m n o p q r s t u v w x y z

abstract kind of art which does not try to show people or things, but instead uses shape and colour to make the picture

architect person who designs buidings

bronze hard shiny metal used in sculpture, made from copper and tin

concertina book book that folds up like the musical instrument called a concertina

Cubism way of painting which shows one thing from different angles or viewpoints

detail small part of a picture

divide separate into two or more parts

landscape picture of natural and man-made scenery, like fields, trees and houses

marble type of stone which many artists like to use for sculpture because it can be made shiny

mosaic	picture or pattern made with small coloured stones or pieces of glass
outline	line which shows the edge and shape of an object
portrait	painting which shows what someone looks like
rectangular	in the shape of a rectangle
repeat	do something over and over again
scene	landscape or view painted by an artist
sculpture	three-dimensional art, made with wood, clay, stone or metal. Can be carved, moulded or glued together.
shade	darker or lighter version of a colour
solid	something which looks like a real, physical object
style	the way in which a picture is painted
triangular	in the shape of a triangle

Index